TALKING
ABOUT THE END
IS ONLY THE
BEGINNING

**Conversations Every Child
Must Have With Their
Aging Parents**

ERIN MARCUS

Talking About the End Is Only the Beginning
Conversations Every Child Must Have With Their Aging Parents
Erin Marcus
MHP Publishing

Published by MHP Publishing, Evanston, Illinois

Printed in the United States of America

Cover and Interior Design: Davis Creative, www.DavisCreative.com

Library of Congress Control Number: 2015908119

ISBN: 978-0-9964253-0-8

ATTENTION CORPORATIONS, UNIVERSITIES, COLLEGES, AND PROFESSIONAL ORGANIZATIONS: Quantity discounts are available on bulk purchases of this book for educational, gift purposes, or as premiums for increasing magazine subscriptions or renewals. Special books or book excerpts can also be created to fit specific needs. For information, please email Erin@ErinMarcus.com.

Table of Contents

Acknowledgements

Thanks to everyone who not just helped me technically write this book, but who supported me in doing so. The people who, when I mentioned I had this idea to take what I have seen over the past 15 years and turn it into something more than just stories, assured me this was a good idea. An idea people would appreciate me sharing. You also reminded me that I could actually accomplish this. And reminded me. And reminded me.

I want to thank Matt Margolis of Margolis Weldon, LLC, whom you will meet later when we start talking about the legal concepts of aging. You have an approach to helping families that I really admire, and I'm excited about your continuing success.

A special thanks to my clients and associates, and my friends and family who provide the stories of my life. I look back at them and am amazed at all the lessons in these stories. They remind me of who I want to be... or, equally importantly, who I do *not* want to be. Hopefully they will help you as well.

And I want to thank my mom, who has been involved in too many of my stories to share here. Hey, Mom—I saw you in the mirror again this morning!

It Only Gets Worse Until You Choose to Make It Better

I hate to be the bearer of bad news, but your parents are getting older. And there's no way to stop it. Things will go on in the coming years... things you need to be prepared for. Decisions must be made. Conversations have to happen—talks you would rather avoid because they make you feel uncomfortable.

How uncomfortable? You'd rather throw away thousands of dollars, and suffer anxiety and heartache than talk to the people who raised you! The people you love. The people who love you.

You're not alone. As the population ages, lots of other adult children are avoiding talking to their parents about the future, too. And the population is aging. According to the U.S. Census Bureau, the number of Americans over the age of 65 is growing by leaps and bounds. In 1980, there were 25.5 million Americans over the age of 65. By 2000, that number had moved up to 35 million. And in 2020, it is projected to reach 56 million.

That is a lot of people to avoid conversations with! What affect is this going to have on our economy? On your family?

Does this sound familiar? Has mom started repeating herself more than normal—but you refuse to believe it's anything more than the fact that she's tired today? Are you worried that if you bring it up, she's going to get mad? Do you think that if you ask about important end-of-life decisions, she'll believe it implies something deeper?

There are a lot of moving parts to all the things you have to discuss with aging parents. Things to keep an eye out for. When should dad no longer be driving—and how do you tell him that? What happens if mom can no longer live in the family home by herself—and where does she go? There are legal ducks to put in a row. There are financial ducks. There are emotional ducks. You're dealing with a whole *flock* of ducks!

This book is for you.

People are living longer. It's normal to have health problems, mobility limitations and need extra help. Modern medicine is turning previously terminal conditions into chronic ones. This is wonderful in many ways, but it also requires more planning than families used to do.

Basically the truth is that people are now living with the conditions and diseases that used to kill them in the good old days.

Equal Time for Dads and Moms

I'll do my best to talk about "dad" as often as I mention "mom." But let's face it: according to research at Harvard University, women outlive men on average by seven years. More often than not, it's either the oldest daughter or the daughter who lives the closest who takes care of mom as she ages.

So this is my chance to specifically acknowledge all the wonderful sons out there who care for their aging parents. The ones who are so worried about the future that they are taking the first step of reading this book. And a shout-out to all their aging fathers as well.

You'll Get Suggestions on How to *Talk*, Not What to *Do*

This book doesn't provide specific legal, medical or financial advice. I'm not here to tell you what your mom's end-of-life wishes *should* be. I'm not going to tell you if you need a traditional will or a revocable trust. Or whether or not to purchase a stand-alone long-term care insurance policy or life insurance with an accelerated death benefit. Or if you should choose to be buried in a cemetery or have your ashes sprinkled on the ivy at Wrigley Field (and how to pull that off without getting arrested!).

I *am* going to tell you that you and your parents have to talk. That you must get comfortable with being uncomfortable. Your family's long-term financial viability and peace of mind depends on this!

Short-Term Avoidance Leads to Long-Term Pain

For more than 15 years—as Senior Vice President of LTCI Partners, the largest insurance brokerage firm in the country focused exclusively on long-term care insurance, and then as Owner of Caring Transitions, Chicago & North Suburbs—I have watched families avoid tough conversations. I have watched them wait too long to purchase long-term care insurance, until they didn't qualify for coverage. (This is like trying to buy homeowners insurance *after* the house burns down!)

I have heard the "Mom can just live with me" response to the topic of aging parents too many times. This is just another avoidance technique, because it doesn't even come close to addressing the other aspects of aging that need to be discussed.

I have witnessed the heartache of hoping that the decisions you made on your father's behalf were the ones he would have wanted. You end up guessing because you never asked him so he never gave you those answers.

And I have watched relationships between siblings fall apart. This happens when families end up in debt due to a lack of planning. Plus they often are at each other's throats because of conflicting views about what mom would have wanted—because nobody bothered to inquire when the chance was there.

3

You Can *Do* This!

I want you to get used to being uncomfortable. I want you to realize how much depends on your ability to do so. And most importantly, I *really* want you to know that it's worth it—for you, your parents, and the rest of your family.

Section 1

WHY

Why Do You Have to Talk to Your Aging Parents
about Their Future *Anyway*?

Chapter 1

Families Go Broke and Experience Horrible Heartache by *Not* Facing and Discussing the Inevitable Facts of Aging

I was visiting an associate at the hospice center where she worked. It's pretty common for this to be a solemn environment, filled with folks who are upset. That day, I saw two sisters who were particularly distraught. They were talking loudly enough for me to overhear as I waited for my friend. Although I tried not to eavesdrop, sometimes it's inevitable.

Interestingly enough, they were not talking about their father's imminent death. They were upset because they realized they had spent the last six months—the final months of their father's life—running around like maniacs trying to get everything in order: finding documents, refiling paperwork, and getting signatures. They had spent all of this time doing everything *except* being with their father!

They can't get that time back.

These women had avoided having a few uncomfortable conversations with their father. They didn't want to make him mad by asking scary questions. They didn't want their questions to *imply* something. They stuck their heads in the sand.

When the inevitable happened—and they could no longer deny it— these grief-stricken daughters had to make all their plans while under duress. They had to guess what dad wanted, instead of knowing. They had to play phone tag with accountants and lawyers and financial advisors, instead of spending time as a family.

Are You Skipping Difficult Conversations in *Other* Parts of Your Life?

Uncomfortable conversations can be about simple things that don't have any real consequences. Let's start with you. Have you ever eaten a bad meal because you didn't want to upset the server who looked really busy? Have you suffered silently with a bad haircut because you didn't want to offend the stylist?

I don't suggest you walk around shouting from the rooftops every time you feel the least bit slighted. But couldn't you have found a nice way to let your feelings be known? Think of it this way. You like doing a good job and making people happy. So does your hair stylist. She can't fix what she didn't know was a problem.

A lot of times it's not *what* we say but *how* we say it. You could have spoken softly and in a neutral tone that showed you were not mad, just not accepting of the haircut. She could have fixed it, and both of you could have been happy with the results.

Maybe you have avoided some conversations with more serious consequences. Have you stayed in a relationship too long because you didn't want to hurt the other person's feelings? You knew she wasn't the one for you, but she was such a nice woman that you didn't want to upset her. Or maybe your girlfriend was so close to your family that you were worried they would be angry if you broke up with her!

What about the time that you didn't speak up about wanting that promotion? You believed this would be scary and confrontational, and it would be *rude* to be so forward. You were the right person for the job, and you knew it. But you didn't want to push your comfort zone, so you gave up a great opportunity. And you actually did the organization a disservice—think of all the progress you could have made toward the company's goals!

Sometimes There Are No Second Chances

Talking to your aging parents about their future is a lot like these types of situations, only with greater consequences. One bad meal isn't the end of the world. And though it may feel like it at the time, neither is an unattractive haircut. Not getting that promotion might have been disappointing, but maybe you went out and got another job rather than have that conversation—you found a way around it.

But with aging parents, there are no "workarounds." And once the opportunity to talk has passed, it's gone.

Just like the two sisters, you don't get that time back.

Watch for "Hiding in the Stuff"

This is another common behavior I've seen. "Hiding in the stuff" happens when the end is near, or my clients have just lost a parent and are not yet ready to really come to grips with it. Instead of facing their feelings, acknowledging how difficult things are and how horrible they feel, they rush around trying to take care of all "the stuff."

I'm pretty good at this one, too. If I take on all the tasks, then I have lots of *other* things to focus on rather than the loss I feel and am trying to avoid. This is just another way of sidestepping the uncomfortable conversation—this time, with yourself. It's hiding from the fear that you feel.

Hiding in the stuff tricks you into thinking that you are actually helping. It makes you feel like you are being productive and useful. But look at this from an outsider's view. Would someone else see it as helping or ignoring the real issues?

You are busy. You have two children who are involved in four different afterschool activities—each—on opposite sides of town. And you have a career. And you have a spouse with his own needs and, oh! who also has parents. I get that. But don't be so busy that you miss this very big deal.

You are not alone. Remember our statistics about the aging population? There are a lot of people going through these same things.

Are Your Parents Like a Frog in Water?

Why don't our *parents* see the changes in their own needs and abilities—rather than needing others to spot them? It's pretty much the old story about the frog in the boiling water. If you put a frog into a pot of water and slowly bring it to a boil, the frog will sit there and not jump out to save itself. (I have not and *will* not be testing this theory.) But if you put a frog into a pot of already boiling water, it will jump right out—of course!

The changes that your parents experience come on so gradually that often *they* don't even see them.

A former co-worker and I were talking. He had been running regularly and now was able to go farther and faster than ever. I don't run. I'm not built for it. I have, however, been involved in power lifting since my teens. At the same time that my coworker was running, I was regularly at the gym and was very pleased with my recent progress.

So there we were, me in my mid-thirties at the time and he in his early forties. My friend mentioned believing he was in the best shape of his life. I thought about it for a moment and then asked, "Oh yeah, how do you get out of bed every morning? Do you jump up like you did when you were a kid, or are those first few steps to the bathroom a little tenuous until your eyes actually focus—or you find your glasses—and you get your feet under you?"

We were laughing. The changes to our bodies were happening so gradually, and we were still so capable in other physical activities, that we were not really aware of the changes that had taken place! Your parents are no different.

How Old Do *You* Feel?

Nobody thinks they're old. I currently think I am 32. (I'm not.) I felt 27 for a long time. Here's how I defined 27: I was on my way in my career, was significantly independent, and had adult relationships (with friends, co-workers, loved ones). But at 27, you're still young enough to enjoy crazy fun nights out with friends, wearing current fashion of any sort, and acting goofy.

A few years ago I moved myself up to 32. I had started to feel more responsible than I would have at 27, and I no longer enjoyed the crazy nights out. I still was playing with fashion, although I probably should have thought that out a little bit better.

If I think about it, I might feel closer to 37. (I'm not.) I should really pay attention to what I wear, so I don't look like I'm going through a mid-life crisis. I can go to a concert and out afterward, but I need to make sure I have nothing to do the next day. In my day-to-day life, I certainly don't feel I am getting older. And it's not until I occasionally look in the mirror and wonder, "Mom! What are you doing in there?" that I even consider that I'm aging.

Your parents are no different. You don't feel old. Why should they?

Fear Can Keep You From Getting Help

Fear also plays a big part in why we avoid hard conversations: our own and with our parents. What emotions are you displaying that could be indicators of fear? And what actions are these emotions keeping you from taking? Here are the common choices.

Denial – "Oh, she's fine." *Really?* "He's not that old yet, so we don't have to worry about anything right now." *Are you sure?* Flat out denial is a difficult barrier to overcome—because it's not based on any logic—so how do you move past it? When planning for the future, this is a dangerous maneuver.

Anger – Have you ever seen someone get mad at a person who could not do something? Maybe they could not hear what was being said to them, and the person being asked to repeat themselves just got more and more angry. You see this a lot when someone is developing indications of dementia and their loved ones respond by saying, "Oh, she's just doing that on purpose!"

Grief – Overwhelming sadness and grief can become paralyzing. Talking to your parents about their future means facing the fact that one day they will no longer be with you. That grief is going to be bad enough when it becomes inevitable. Why bring it on any sooner? So you just avoid the whole situation.

Guilt – You know you should be doing more to help dad now that he is living alone at home. You know you should be spending more time with him. But you have two kids and a job and you live 90 minutes away. So you feel guilty over not doing what you think you should be doing. Getting someone to help do some of the things that need to be done is an admission of the fact that you are not doing them yourself. You don't want to feel that guilt, so you avoid the issue altogether.

Here's the truth. By talking to your parents about what *they* want to have happen, and planning for it, you get to focus on being a *family*. Then you don't have to be a doctor, a lawyer, an accountant, a social director, a barrier-free interior decorator, and a home health care assistant. You get to stop being all the things you *don't* actually know how to be. But you will always be your parents' advocate.

Key Questions From Chapter 1:

- What conversations are you avoiding because you're afraid of being uncomfortable?

  - Which of these conversations are of little consequence?

  - Which of these conversations are more serious?

- Are you so busy that you absolutely cannot devote the time to these important conversations, or are you just hiding out?

  - What emotions, including fear, are keeping you from facing the future head on?

Chapter 2

The Stakes Are Just Too High If You *Don't* Speak Up

When I was five, an accident with the family dog resulted in me getting nipped in the face. Unfortunately, I was a small five-year-old and the dog was a 150+-pound Great Dane. My parents took me to the emergency room, where the attending physician wanted to put my face back together. My mother wouldn't let him. She made sure I was no longer in imminent danger, and then we waited three hours for one of the best plastic surgeons in the area to get to the hospital and do the job.

Because my mother stepped up—and didn't just let things happen without her input—you can barely tell I had 110 stitches in my face. Look at the picture on the back cover. Amazing, right?

What if my mother just let things happen without asking if there was a better choice? Would I have survived if the ER doctor repaired the damage to my face instead of waiting for the specialist? Of course. But the outcome would have been very different, because the emergency room doctor did not have the special plastic surgery skills that the specialist did or the vested interest in me that my mother did.

Giving Control to Someone Else—Like the Government

It's not okay to just let things happen. The stakes are too high if you don't speak up. It is *not* okay to let people without a vested interest in your life—or your parents' lives—make decisions because you wouldn't step up and take responsibility; because you wouldn't be proactive.

It's easier when you have people to blame. You can avoid the hard work, skip the uncomfortable conversation, and then have an excuse to say it wasn't your fault. It was society's fault. It was the government's fault. It was your brother's fault. (OK, maybe that one is true…) But who is the one who loses here? Who is the one living with the heartache? You.

And then there are the *legalities* of not having conversations with your parents about their future, and what they want to happen. Every state has a probate process for the money and personal belongings of someone who has passed.

Take a moment to digest that.

Think of the government and how the people who work there do things… now think of them in charge of your mother's estate. How efficient are they going to be? They certainly won't be working on your timetable, or take into account what family members say they want to have happen. By then, it's too late for that input. And, of course, there are the potential tax implications. It's a pretty safe bet that the state's plan for handling an estate is not going to consider keeping your taxes as low as possible.

The Simple Power of Asking

One thing that always surprises me is how often, when you ask your parents about some aging-related topics, they actually have a fairly concrete idea of what they want. It's just that nobody ever talked with them about it!

I guess they're not called the Silent Generation for nothing. You can't assume that if your parents had plans they would just tell you. Oddly enough, sometimes they think you just automatically *know* what they want—in the same way that you think they would speak up if they had plans!

It could end up being one of those situations where the pain and fear leading up to the event is infinitely worse then the event itself. Like getting a shot from the doctor. You are nervous about it, but the entire ordeal lasts only a few seconds, and it doesn't really hurt that much.

Imagine if you asked your father where he wants to live if he can no longer stay in the family home. And not only can he answer that question, but he already has the answers to 80 percent of the *other* questions you have for him. Think of all the time you spent needlessly worrying!

A lot of times your parents are just waiting for someone to ask. But you don't, because the entire subject makes you uncomfortable. And they won't volunteer the information because you *didn't* ask.

And there you both sit, in a mutual stalemate.

My dad had plans I didn't know about. I was helping him move several years ago. Sitting on the floor in the living room, packing the items from the bookcase, I picked up a very heavy, nondescript brown metal box. "What's in here?" I asked. He said, "The dog." Seriously: it was his dog's ashes.

Then he told me he wanted to be cremated, have his ashes mixed with the dog's, and sprinkled in their favorite woods. I said, "Okay, but how was I supposed to know this if you didn't tell me?"

Maybe it would have come up another time. Being me, eventually I would have talked to him about the subject. But if that series of events didn't happen, would he have spoken up? What do your parents already know they want to do that they haven't mentioned to you?

Conversations That Protect Your Parents

Driving

Driving—and when to stop driving—is one of the more difficult conversations that has to happen. Some people are wonderfully well aware that they can no longer see as well or no longer react as well. Though it may be difficult, they proactively decide to stop driving. Other times it's not so easy.

Like so many other topics that have to be discussed with our aging parents, driving is *not* just about driving. It's about independence. It's about not having to rely on other people for simple requirements, such as just going to the grocery store or the pharmacy.

Often someone will decide they just won't drive very far anymore, or they are OK if they stay off the highway. But statistics show that one out of three accidents happen within one mile of where a person lives. One mile! It's where people are so comfortable that maybe they're not paying as much attention as they otherwise would.

Many times the misadventures of an elderly driver are told in almost cartoon-like fashion. We joke lightly about how dad suddenly got turned around coming home from his local grocery store, or scraped the inside of the garage wall. And, sure dad may be embarrassed about the incident, but thankfully, the challenges that occur seldom end up as a terrible tragedy. They are just a mere inconvenience for the driver who gets lost, or the family who is out looking for him. But this frivolous tone disappears quickly when the results are something more devastating.

This is one of those topics where *mindset* is a very big issue. It's understandable that dad doesn't want to give up his independence after having been in charge of his family for 50 years. However, the truth of the matter is that its not just *dad* who is at risk here. It is every other person on the road, or on the sidewalk, or in the parking lot he may be driving through.

Imagine the effect on the family if dad were to be seriously injured in a car crash he caused. Or worse: how many news stories have you read where a person hit the gas instead of the brake and killed someone?

We have two different high-stakes risks here. The obvious one is your parent, who is injured in an accident. Let's assume for argument's sake that dad is not injured in an accident. What about his *emotional* state? How does your amazing father live with himself after causing an accident where somebody is hurt? Or worse?

I can't even fathom the strain of knowing that something I did caused that amount of destruction to another person, and to their family. I certainly don't want my father experiencing that! Especially if it was something I could have influenced if only I had not been so uncomfortable with the conversation that I didn't bring it up.

Money

One of the benefits of being actively involved in your parent's lives is that you can head off some decisions that might not be made in their best interests. Often this involves finances.

If money is a taboo subject in your family, there's a greater chance that your parents will be taken advantage of. There are a lot of highly educated, fully capable older adults who are very good at taking care of their finances. But here's the truth. A lot of people are just looking for the opportunity to take advantage of an unsuspecting senior.

Unfriendly "Friends"

Research has shown that just as our brains are not fully able to calculate risk until our early 20s (explains a lot, doesn't it?) after age 60, often the brain is less able to identify when people are trying to take advantage of us. Biologically speaking, we are more gullible.

It doesn't have to be an email from some prince in Nigeria claiming he can only get to his millions—which he is willing to share with you—if you will just send him enough money to cover the fees involved. It is often much more subtle.

It's the "friend" who, at 30 years younger than your mom, is making sure that her sidewalk is shoveled, and runs to the store for her. That might be wonderful. But what if that friend needs a place to stay all of a sudden, and then his car breaks down and needs a costly repair? Should your mom be loaning him money and letting him stay in the extra room? Maybe. Maybe that person is also on his own and the two of them have a nice friendship. But make sure it doesn't cross the line into manipulative and abusive behavior.

Some of these situations really aren't abusive and the "friend" does truly help. But then mom needs to move out of the house because she can't walk up the stairs anymore, and the "friend" has to find his own place to live and pay his own bills. Suddenly things aren't so friendly anymore.

My client Bertha was one of the most amazing, talented and well-traveled people I've met. She was also a drama queen and a hoarder. Yes: it was one of those situations you see on TV, where you can just walk through little paths in a couple of rooms. The dust was bad. Now her failing health and eyesight were forcing her to move out of her home.

Luckily for Bertha, most of what she collected was actually cool stuff—once we dug it out. And her estate sale was going to result in some nice profits for her.

There was a man, Tim, who helped Bertha and even stayed with her from time to time. He would go to the store for her, shovel her walk and drive her places. When I first met Tim, he was very nice and legitimately concerned about Bertha. She wasn't in financial duress, and her own children lived some distance away, so it was good to have Tim around the house.

Then Tim realized Bertha was moving out of the house he where he could stay for free whenever he wanted. Where he kept his car in the garage for free. Where she paid for the meals they ate. And to top it off, she wasn't going to take him up on his offer of hiring him to clear her house for her, sell all the wonderful pieces she wasn't keeping, and help her move to her new assisted living community.

He was losing his free ride and the income from a job he felt she owed him. Over the course of about a week, Tim changed drastically. I noticed the stronger smell of alcohol each time I ran into him. He tried to use his size to intimidate me, and hover over my five-foot frame when discussions turned to who would be doing what for Bertha going forward. Tim was scared—and getting scary. Within 10 days of moving Bertha, the locks had to be changed on the house to prevent the stealing and damage we were starting to see.

Even good situations can turn bad when people feel threatened. Being involved in your parents finances and lives from the beginning will lessen the likelihood of these situations.

Wishes for Their Care

Take a minute to slow down. Remember that story at the beginning of Chapter 1? The one about the sisters who spent the last six months of their father's life running around taking care of things that should have been addressed years before? I want to add a particularly important point to that story.

If you talk to your parents about what they want to have happen, what they tell you can be one of the best gifts of your life.

It is the gift of *knowing* versus *hoping.*

When you speak with your parents about their future, once they are gone, you spend the rest of your life knowing you did the right thing, instead of hoping you did. What affect would that have on you?

Don't underestimate the pride you get to share when you talk to your children about your own future. The pride in knowing that you set an example for them by approaching a difficult situation head-on and taking care of your family—instead of hiding your head in the sand.

One of the most important things you need to know is to what extreme mom wishes you to go in regards to end-of-life life saving measures.

This is one of those times where planning and knowing ahead of time is going to save you more heartache than you will already be going through. Because you already know what mom wants, you can just act on it instead of worrying if it is the right thing to do.

My mom and I have very similar opinions about to what extreme measures should be taken regarding end of life efforts. The bottom line for us: if we are already old and sick and life-saving efforts will not improve our quality of life but just keep us technically alive for a short period of time, don't do it.

At the risk of offending some of you, it breaks my heart to watch people suffer as, at 85-years-old, they are kept barely alive by artificial means. People do to their parents what I would not allow my dog to go through! Whose benefit are you really considering when this happens? Will you let your fear and dread over losing your mom prolong her suffering? I am not by any means discounting your very real emotions. I ask you to consider who you are looking out for when you make these decisions: yourself or your mother?

My grandma died after a series of heart attacks. It seems to me this happened rather quickly over a week or two. She wasn't feeling well, went into the hospital, came home, went back to the hospital, and started to have heart attacks. After being notified that things suddenly turned serious, my mom flew to Florida to be with my grandma. She went straight from the airport to the hospital.

As nurses and doctors being used to saving lives, the staff at the hospital kept reviving my grandma. That is what they are trained to do: something goes wrong and they fix it.

At one point my mother physically stood between my grandma and the doctor and told them, "Don't you dare touch her again." She knew how it was going to end. She knew that grandma was too sick to ever really get better.

How painful is it to be brought back from the brink only to tip over again? I don't know. But if it is even a tiny bit painful, and it is not going to solve anything, why should grandma have to endure it?

It is something I happen to feel strongly about. If you *know* that the end is inevitable, I would rather let someone go one month too early than one day of suffering too late.

You don't have to agree with me. You can go in completely the opposite direction and say that you want absolutely every measure to be taken at every possible moment to prolong your life. What your decision is, and how you want to approach it, is not what I am concerned about. I just want to make sure that you know your *parents'* opinions.

My mom knows how I feel. I know how she feels. And it will be hard and horrible and devastating if and when the time comes for me to make these decisions. But I take a lot of comfort in knowing that I will make the right ones. And I will make them because I already know what she wants me to do.

Key Questions From Chapter 2

- Are you making the decisions in your life that should only be made by people personally vested in your wellbeing? Are your parents?

- Are you worrying needlessly because your parents have information they didn't share and you didn't ask about?

- Are you aware enough of your parents' lives to make sure they are not being taken advantage of?

- Once your parents are gone, will you get to spend the rest of your life knowing you did what they would have wanted, instead of just hoping that you did?

Chapter 3

Waiting Reduces Options
and Makes Them More Expensive

Have you ever planned a vacation and forgotten to buy the plane tick-et—even when you put it on your to-do list? Or worse: a sudden opportunity came up and you had to get halfway across the country to-morrow? Plane tickets get very expensive the longer you wait. Most of the flights are full, so you might have to take the red-eye… or a flight with an otherwise avoidable layover. Waiting reduces your options and makes them more expensive.

This does not just apply to air travel.

The World Doesn't Turn on a Dime—It Takes Big Bucks

I get a handful of calls each year from families that have waited too long. They tell me their parent's house has sold, is closing at the end of the week, and they would like to have an estate sale for the unwanted items. Or that the closing on the house happens in two days, and they would like help arranging for a charity to pick up the remaining household goods.

Seriously: didn't they know this was coming? What do they think can be done in two days? With few exceptions, there is no way they decided to sell their parents' home, found a realtor, did the paperwork, got it listed, had a showing, received a bid, accepted the bid, had buyers go through the entire mortgage process, and everyone received a closing date—all within four days.

This did not sneak up on anybody.

By waiting, they no longer have the option of an estate sale that can get the house ready for closing with no out-of-pocket costs, and also earn the family a bit of a profit. Instead, they have to pay a company to remove everything from the house. And while items will still go to a charity, the bill for the service will be in the thousands of dollars. Instead of *making* money, they have to *spend* money because they didn't plan.

Plan, Don't React

Waiting until the last minute is always going to be more expensive or give you inferior results than you would receive by planning ahead.

What creates a better financial retirement plan? You can start out by saving money in a 401(k) when you are 35 and continue to invest over a lifetime, or you can wait until you are 65 and see how much money you can scrape together to buy an annuity.

Spontaneity is the spice of life to many people, and I am definitely one of them. I have no idea what I am going to eat for dinner most evenings, because I don't know what I am going to feel like eating until I'm hungry. The downside is that often, not having planned for an actual meal, I end up eating a series of foods that may or may not be related to each other—versus what most people would consider a healthy meal.

There are times when spontaneity is just not the answer.

Don't Get Hung up On "Plan A"

During my time at LTCI Partners, I traveled the country making presentations to financial planners on the importance of long-term care insurance for their clients.

One December, I was on the road with John, the Director of Insurance for a large regional bank. We were giving presentations to local offices. There was some pushback from some of the agents who complained that they didn't like to recommend long-term care. This wasn't because they didn't believe in the product—it was because they felt it was difficult for their clients to get approved. The agents didn't like going back to their clients and giving them bad news that they had been declined for coverage.

John had the best response I had ever heard to that objection.

He told the agents that they just became the most important person in their client's life. That the insurance companies—with all of their research and actuaries and formulas—had basically said their client was a bad risk. They were practically guaranteeing that this person was going to have a long-term care need in the future. And if long-term care insurance was *not* the right solution for this client, then the financial planner had better find *another* one.

John understood the need for planning instead of reacting. He knew it was important that the first version of the plan not be the *only* version. And when the stakes are this high, you didn't give up because your initial approach didn't work.

Having *Some* Kind of Plan Is Important

Maybe dad didn't qualify for long-term care insurance. Or maybe he just doesn't like it. There are several financial products from highly-rated companies that will provide money in the event that someone needs long-term care. But what if dad didn't buy *any* of them—and now the only way he can afford to move into an assisted living community is to sell the house?

What did this lack of planning cost the family?

Investing a couple thousand dollars a year could have provided a long-term care plan. So could a life insurance policy with an accelerated benefit. Leveraging the money in any of several ways could have earned enough money to provide options.

Instead, the family home has to go. And it needs to be sold immediately, because dad is sick and can't move back home after getting out of the hospital because the only full bathroom is on the second floor. And you end up having to take the first offer because dad needs the cash now. Is this what your dad wanted for his legacy?

Medicare does not cover long-term care needs. Sometimes selling the family home is the only option to cover these costs. If that's the case, then this is the right thing to do. But maybe it could have been avoided had you planned ahead.

Your Own Planning for Your Parent's Future

As your parents age, there is a real chance that you will have to make adjustments to your own life as well. Talking about things early means you can make plans for how to handle these changes instead of reacting to them when they pop up.

What if you decide that mom will come to live with you? You probably will need to make some physical changes to your home. Wouldn't it be nice to plan those properly, and do them in a way that adds value to the house and comfort for your family—instead of throwing things out of a back den and into storage while mom is in rehab after knee surgery, and you have six days to get a room ready for her?

And if there are grandchildren involved, planning can be even more important. It's unfair to expect your children to adjust instantly to a drastic change in their living arrangements and schedule. They may have to give up their own rooms and begin sharing, or lose the family room where they spend time with their friends.

If you are lucky then these new living arrangements could mean that grandma is home every day when the kids get home from school and welcomes them with the all-American plate of cookies and glass of milk. But what if grandma needs care and you are no longer able to welcome them home every day in quite the same fashion as before, because of adjustments to *your* schedule?

Helping everyone prepare in advance for these types of transitions can go a long way to preserving the peace. It also makes having an extended family together under one roof an amazing experience instead of a burden.

No Longer Being Allowed to Decide

There is something else you need to be aware of about waiting too long to plan. Events can happen that make it no longer legally possible for your parents to decide for themselves.

- More than 5 million Americans are living with Alzheimer's Disease.

- Every 67 seconds, someone in the United States develops Alzheimer's.

- Almost two-thirds of Americans with Alzheimer's are women.

One of the biggest surprises to me as I began to work with people with varying levels of dementia—and also experience it within members of my own family—is that people are very good at hiding this condition at first.

For families that don't live near each other, it's even easier to *not* see the signs. The quick weekly phone call with mom often starts with "How are you doing?" to which she replies, "Fine." Then she asks questions about you and your kids. You're used to that process, because it started when you first went off to kindergarten and came home to the question, "What did you do today?" So you just tell her what's going on in your life and with her grandchildren.

Mom makes short comments but no real conversation, and you don't realize that something isn't quite right. And she doesn't want to worry you—or *she* doesn't want to have an uncomfortable conversation—so mom doesn't tell you that she knows something isn't quite right.

The holidays come around. The family travels across the country to visit mom for a few days. Now you realize some things aren't being taken care of the way they should be. The way they used to be. So you decide to get your ducks in a row.

You contact the family attorney to set up a review. Your parents have always been good planners, and there were a lot of documents prepared at some point—before you had your children, and before your oldest brother became an unfortunate challenge for the family.

Here's the problem. The attorney spends a fair amount of time with mom and also realizes that something is not quite right. He ultimately decides that mom is not legally capable of making the desired changes to the documents that were so carefully crafted 17 years ago. And now you are stuck with either keeping plans that you no longer want, or a potential legal battle to try to change them.

Planning is not a one and done affair. Like you and your parents, it requires regular checkups to make sure a small problem doesn't turn into a dire situation.

Key Questions From Chapter 3

- This is not the time for spontaneity. If you don't have a plan, what will this cost your family?

- Don't get confused between the *goal* of the plan and how to *get* there. Can you have a Plan B?

- Are you making sure that the plans you and your parents want in place are updated and current in case something happens that makes it impossible to change them?

Section 2

HOW

You're Sold on "Why."
Let's Talk about *How* You Do This!

Chapter 4

You Don't Always Have to Be Sad or Serious—Humor Helps

My mother pre-purchased her funeral. An older gentleman came over when mom was in her mid-50s and I in my mid-30s to go over the details of what she wanted. One of her wishes was a headstone with a little locket-like panel attached, where you put a picture. She even knew which picture she wanted. It's one from her wedding to my stepdad—and I agree it's a beautiful photo. But I didn't want one specific image representing her in my memory.

We went back and forth about it. Then—much to the horror of the nice gentleman trying to help us—I came up with a plan. I told mom she could have the locket feature on the headstone on one condition. Before she died, we were going to arrange for a photo shoot. We would bring a few different Halloween costumes. Have some beach shots in different bathing suits. Maybe dress her up as cupid for Valentine's Day. Have a fun formal outfit for New Year's Eve. We would turn the little locket photo idea into a calendar and have enough pictures to change them out each month for a few years.

I thought it was genius! Mom laughed. The cemetery rep just giggled nervously.

Here's the thing. Don't use humor to avoid the import conversations that need to take place and the planning that needs to be done. Instead, know that part of the avoidance is the fear, and one of the antidotes of fear is humor.

Humor is How You Celebrate Life

Consider the different ways you celebrate life's big events. Now, think of the most memorable versions of those events. Whether it's a Hollywood awards show, a graduation commencement speech, or even a eulogy at a funeral. More likely than not, the times that stand out the most to you are the ones that involved humor.

I have worked with many families who recently lost a loved one. By far, the experiences that have touched me the most are where the fond memories were shared through humorous stories. Those are the people I felt I knew best—even if I never got to meet them before they passed.

I once saw an article that listed the ways that humor can heal:

1. Humor combats fear
2. Humor comforts
3. Humor relaxes
4. Humor reduces pain
5. Humor boosts the immune system
6. Humor reduces stress
7. Humor spreads happiness
8. Humor cultivates optimism
9. Humor helps communication

Chances are good that you'll need it to do *all* of these things.

William Arthur Ward, one of America's most quoted authors of inspirational sayings, once wrote, "A well developed sense of humor is the pole that adds balance to your steps as you walk the tightrope of life." Let's face it: there are few scarier tightropes than contemplating and planning for your aging parent's future.

A Sense of Humor in the Face of Difficulty

It's amazing what effect humor can have on quality of life. Or even just the ability to not take everything so seriously.

My client, Ellen, had some serious problems with dementia. It was all associated with her short-term memory. We would meet at her condo, with her daughter-in-law Julie, to get ready to move her to a memory care community. Usually I would wait for Julie downstairs in the parking lot, and we would go inside together.

One day, Julie was stuck in traffic. She called and suggested I go upstairs on my own. Maybe Ellen would remember me. And even if she didn't, I wasn't exactly a threatening presence.

Ellen let me in and asked me why I was there. I reminded her we were working together on helping her move. She did remember she was moving—so far so good.

We sat at the kitchen table and she asked me, "Do you need me to show you around or did we already do that?" She didn't even hesitate or care that she may have forgotten what we had done before. I told her we already looked around and were just going to finalize the plans.

Julie arrived, and Ellen got up to let her in. They walked back into the kitchen. Ellen saw me and said, "This person is here. I don't remember her name or why she's here, but I think we are having a nice time."

She had a sense of humor about her situation. She wasn't going to let what most people think of as their worst nightmare have a negative impact on her daily life.

I loved it!

The movie "Parenthood" has a scene with Steve Martin and Mary Steenburgen arguing over his need for control and her desire for him to relax and go with the flow. Steve is annoyed with everything. His grandmother, overhearing them, talks about her love of going on roller coasters—versus others who ride the merry-go-round and just go in circles. That it is the ups and downs in life that make it all interesting. Then she leaves to wait for them in the car. Mary goes on a rant about how wonderful his grandmother's perspective is. To which Steve replies, "If she is so brilliant, how come she is sitting in the neighbor's car?"

Just because some things are becoming more challenging, don't discount everything that your parents have to offer.

It can't all be a joke. Have some good factual information about options and what worries you, so they know you are serious. Use humor as a way to break the ice, start the conversation and lighten the mood.

Key Questions From Chapter 4

- Humor helps in difficult situations—but do you know the difference between using humor as a tool, and joking around as a way to avoid a situation?

- Can you find a way, maybe an "inside joke" to share with your siblings, as a reminder to keep your senses of humor through what could a difficult process?

- What can you learn from someone else's approach to life and their ability to use humor?

Chapter 5

Family Dynamics Explode
If You Ignore Them

David was the executor of his parents' estate. His mother had already passed, and he had just lost his father. The family home had sold, and we were going to hold an estate sale to get the house ready for closing. I first met with David to go over the details. Then we thought it best for me to meet his sisters as well, so everyone would be comfortable with the plan.

In a very nice voice as I walked in, David said, "Erin, this is my sister Rachel. And this is my sister Susan, who I get along with." It was awesome! Here was a highly successful, grown businessman who couldn't pass up the opportunity to take a dig at his little sister. I love the way he did it too.

Technically, he never said anything bad about her—he never said *anything* about her! If I had been with them for any other reason than handling their father's estate, David would have never felt compelled to make that comment.

What is it about dealing with our parents that turns us back into children?

Having Our *Own* Second Childhood

One of the interesting things about having conversations with aging parents is how all the unresolved sibling rivalries from when you were eight years old bubble to the surface. All the civility and peacefulness that your family has created so you can endure Thanksgiving dinner together goes right out the window.

I was working with another family. While we were in the process of helping mom downsize, things took a turn for the worse. It became clear that she would never get the chance to move into the independent living community. There were three siblings: a sister and two brothers, one of whom lived across the country. Luckily, the brother made it home to visit mom in the hospital one last time. She passed within hours of his arrival.

After her death, the sister went straight from the hospital to the family home. She gathered all of the items that she wanted to keep. She didn't give her brothers or the extended family the time to even digest what was happening or to make decisions as a family.

Would she have been able to keep all the "stuff" she seemed so anxious to have if she had spoken with everyone else first? Probably. But as the youngest child who had always felt ignored by her older brothers, she jumped the gun before they could stop her. You know she would have never done that if a group of her friends were involved instead of her older brothers. I wonder what the lasting effects of her actions had on the family dynamics.

Knowing the relationships among people in a family can be very helpful before you head into these conversations. Take a mental inventory of what you anticipate happening and from whom. Are all the siblings on the same page? The fear from siblings and how this manifests itself can derail this whole effort.

And sometimes if you are lucky, these types of conversations and situations can bring people closer together.

Creating Stronger Relationships

One family I worked had two sisters living on opposite sides of the country. They were working to help dad move closer to one of them. Each month, we would get together for about a week to take the next steps in this big move, with its dozens of variables.

These sisters got along with each other. There were no weird dynamics, and things were moving along just fine. The beauty in this particular instance was watching a new relationship form between them. Each of the two adults appreciated the strengths and the differences the other brought to the situation. By being mature, with each understanding that the other was working hard and making sacrifices, they created a family bond much stronger than just having grown up in the same household.

I worked with another set of siblings on an estate sale for their mother. We always met as a group and everyone copied all the other parties on emails. There wasn't any indication that this had been anything other than a nice loving family. About half way through the work, I had a conversation with the sister. Turns out that she and her brother had been estranged for years over a family business-related issue. But when they lost mom, and as they came together to take care of the estate, they realized what they had been missing in not speaking to each other for so long. And what their children had been missing. And that it was time to change this.

I don't know that they ever became the "warm fuzzy holiday dinner all in one room" type of family, but I do know they both felt lucky to be reunited as a family.

Birth—and Pecking—Order

Birth order can play an interesting role when caring for a parent—even more so when it's time to divide the estate.

Oldest children often think they should automatically be in charge, because they always have been. Then the favorites think they should direct things, because they know what dad "really" wanted to happen. The middle children are angry about being ignored—again. Everyone is mad at the youngest ones because they always got more, and already received plenty of handouts. And nobody is going to listen to them anyway.

Hopefully with age comes a softening of the hierarchy of your youth—or at least the ability to consider what your siblings also are going through as they watch your parents get older.

Having conversations with your parents about what they would like to have happen *while* they age can go along way in preserving sibling relationships. Instead of all the infighting, and claims that one person knows more than the others about what mom wants, mom can just tell you. When those conversations *don't* happen, and siblings are left to make decisions on their own, many underlying problems only intensify.

How do the in-laws in the family come into play? Sometimes the closest female relative to mom is a daughter-in-law. Often she becomes the automatic caregiver. Or if there are no daughters and only sons, the same dynamic holds true: it's a daughter-in-law doing much of the caregiving. I have seen too many examples of a daughter-in-law depended upon to be the primary care giver as dad needs help, but when it's time to make decisions or disperse belongings, that same daughter-in-law is now excluded from the family discussions.

Figuring out who the "right" people are to have involved can be more challenging than it first appears. Maybe it's not quite as obvious as it seems. (In the next chapter, I'm going to remind you to remember your intentions as your family all comes together.)

What happens if you involve stepchildren? Here we go... and the spouses of stepchildren?

Now the "Who should be involved?" question becomes as clear as mud.

A note of caution: You can't do everything by consensus. It can start out with the best intentions. Everyone is on the same page, but it's probably because the decisions to be made are minor at this point and mom is still really in charge of most of it. As the choices become more difficult, you realize that everyone being involved in every conversation and every decision becomes a logistical nightmare. Even with texting and email, you realize that leadership by committee is not all its cracked up to be.

One of my favorite office-related quotes applies here as well: "When *everybody* is responsible for something, then *nobody* is responsible for it!"

Want to know a sure-fire way to really piss off your siblings in this situation? Be the person who wants to make all the decisions but not do any of the work—or pay for any of it.

Noticing Role Reversals

An interesting dynamic happens in many families as parents age. The aging parents start to defer what look like very easy everyday decisions to their children.

I was working with Esther and her mother. We were walking through mom's house, room by room, deciding what to bring with to her new apartment at an independent living community. Every time I asked mom if she wanted to keep something, she would have the same reply. She looked at Esther and asked her if she wanted it.

After this had gone on for a while, Esther started repeating the question back to her mom with increasing annoyance, "Do *you* want to keep this?"

Mom would answer, "Only if *you* don't want it." And round and round we went.

I eventually took Esther off to the side and told her just to lie. "For everything except the stuff you definitely want to keep, just tell mom, 'No, I don't want it.'" This was the best way we could get mom to make a decision based on *her* wants and needs and not her daughter's. It was also the only way we were going to get ready to move on time!

I often wondered why some older adults defer even easy decisions. As I paid more attention, the more this appeared to be about the family's overall dynamic—and not so much the accepted wisdom that eventually the child has to parent the parent.

Unless a medical condition dictates otherwise, there should be no role reversal. Of course things change, and mom is going to need you to help her in ways you did not before. But she is not a child. The best situation would be for your relationship with your mother to have matured into a mutually respectful adult peer-to-peer situation.

Now, before you start clearing your throat at me, I said "best," not "most likely."

Children with the best intentions often step in to help parents. However, sometimes maybe what you should be doing is *asking*, not *telling*. Also let the parents help themselves. When a parent hovers over their children throughout their lives—not letting them make their own mistakes and their own decisions—children often end up as insecure adults who don't have the confidence to succeed on their own. Taking over for your parent may not have quite the same impact, but it is still not always in their best interest.

To skew a quote once made by Abraham Lincoln for our own purposes here, "You cannot help men by doing for them what they can and should do for themselves."

Benefits of a Neutral Third Party in Difficult Conversations

One of the things that can ease challenging family dynamics is the addition of a neutral third party. We're *not* referring to those cases where all three siblings have their own lawyers and are already threatening to sue each other over who gets to keep every trinket in the house. (Yes, unfortunately, those families exist.)

I'm referring to situations where all family members really *do* have the best intentions. These siblings are probably in general agreement with each other on what they want to see happen as dad ages. But they are so nervous about having these conversations that they can't get the ball rolling. Or maybe—even if after you have read this book and you are committed to giving it a try—you're not quite sure where to start.

The neutral third party could come in a variety of forms. This could be your parent's lawyer or accountant, who has been working with them for years. Or a geriatric care manager. Or maybe it's someone who understands the challenges of these types of conversations and has created a safe, comfortable environment for doing this.

The neutral third party can offer more than subject matter expertise on things. Sometimes it just takes the presence of a responsible adult who is *not* a member of the family to keep everyone *else* acting like responsible adults. If the only benefit is to remind everyone that none of them is six years old any more, then—quite honestly—this will help your family.

Key Questions From Chapter 5

- While attempting to keep childhood issues at bay, take a moment to consider the dynamics in your family. Are you all on the same page?

- Remember: leading by committee may sound good in the beginning but can become a nightmare. Can you divide and conquer the tasks here?

- Are you noticing any tendencies toward role reversals between you and your parents that shouldn't be there?

- Would bringing in a neutral third party help?

Chapter 6

This Will Be Hard

Be a Hero

D r. Phil McGraw, the popular self-help expert, makes a point that's really useful here. "Every situation needs a hero."

There are a lot of complex family dynamics and some real fears that go with talking to your aging parents about their futures. The first time you try this, there's a good chance things won't go well. Dad may get defensive, or mom may lay down some heavy guilt. Or your big brother, who thinks he is in charge, may sabotage the whole thing. That's OK. Part of the reason this is such a big problem in our society is because it is just not easy.

Listen to Dr. Phil. Keep at it. Show your intentions. You want to make sure your parents are well taken care of, and they have everything they want and need. You are not trying to take anything away from them or your siblings: you just want to make sure that the family ducks are in a row.

If you *don't* have your parent's interests truly at heart, it will show and none of this will work.

Being a hero is often harder than it sounds under the best circumstances, let alone once you add in the emotions of family dynamics and the fear of your parents getting older. Be prepared to have to try this more than once.

Take personal responsibility for the situation. Decide you are going to make sure that the right thing happens. And don't confuse what you want to see happen with what mom wants!

Watch for Generational Differences

I'm going to throw another curve in here. These conversations involve more than one generation, and each one has different characteristics that add to the challenge.

If you Google "generational differences," you will see pages of information. While most entries have to do with the workplace, many of these characteristics come into play for our topic as well. Although each generation raised the next, the environment where this happened made them very different.

The Greatest Generation

The Greatest Generation/The Silent Generation was born before 1946. They experienced the Great Depression, the New Deal, World War II, and the atomic bomb. They were taught to be hard workers and savers, to follow the rules and respect authority.

My client, Franny, was downsizing from a very large condo to a one-bedroom apartment in an independent living community. She was a great planner and very active. She wanted everything done on her terms before she couldn't make those decisions on her own. My kind of woman!

As we were walking through her condo, looking at the furniture that would best fit in her new home, Franny mentioned not wanting to take two particular end tables from the living room. She was emphatic that they were absolutely *not* coming with her, and she was happy to be rid of them.

I asked her about the ill will toward the tables. Franny told me that her mother gave her those tables as hand-me-downs when she was first married, and every time she moved she knew she had to keep them. She had hated them since the day they showed up.

I said, "Franny, you are 93 years old! Why in the world haven't you gotten rid of these before?" She told me that her mother said that her father had worked hard to buy those tables. She needed to keep them. So she had kept them—until now.

Baby Boomers

Baby Boomers were born between 1946 and 1964. They experienced the Civil Rights movement, space travel, the Cold War, the sexual revolution, and some significant assassinations. They have a more optimistic viewpoint, and value teamwork, personal growth, involvement and personal gratification.

Some of my favorite clients are the Boomer snowbirds who finally decided to give up the house in Chicago and just keep the one in Florida. They are so happy to leave with the clothes on their back and maybe a few favorite items. They already have a fully furnished house waiting for them. As long as the job is done well, they barely care about the details. They can't wait to get back to their book clubs and dance classes in the Sunshine State.

Generation X

Generation Xers were born between 1965 and 1976. Their world was shaped by Watergate, the Iran hostage crisis, the fall of the Berlin Wall, Operation Desert Storm, and the Women's Liberation movement. They were the latchkey kids. They tend to be more cynical then previous generations, and value fun and informality along with independence and self-reliance.

This generation doesn't want to be too tied to anything. Most of what they have is temporary and transportable. If something isn't sold at Target, nobody needs it. If the DVD player breaks, there's no need to fix it—just buy a new one. It's cheaper, and odds are the technology has changed anyway. The idea of "fixing" instead of replacing anything smaller than a car is just crazy.

The World in a Dining Room Set

Here is where things get tricky.

Picture a beautiful, if not gigantic, dining room set in solid mahogany. This was not cheap! Back in the day, not only did the father of the young family work hard to finally purchase the set—with cash, not credit—but it was a rite of passage piece as well.

Buying this furniture meant that the young family could start hosting Thanksgiving dinner instead of going to their parents' houses for holidays. They were officially adults. The two-piece hutch with the beveled glass doors held the set of china that was purchased, again with cash, as their wedding present from a group of aunts and uncles. The china has gold metal trim, which came long before the invention of the dishwasher or microwave oven.

Fast-forward 60 years. Dad is gone. Mom is getting ready to move to a single story condo so she doesn't have to walk up and down stairs, or worry about the lawn and the snow removal. She is concerned about what to do with the dining room set and the beautiful contents of the hutch. It won't fit in the new condo.

The 58-year-old daughter does not want it. She already has her own, if slightly smaller, set. The 35-year-old granddaughter doesn't want it. She has a corporate job, a husband who travels for work, and a young son who is already enrolled in three different afterschool activities at age five. If the china doesn't go in the microwave and dishwasher, this young family doesn't have time to take care of it. Tastes in décor have changed as well.

How do they tell grandma that her rite of passage dining room set that grandpa was so proud to have purchased for her has no place in their lives?

Isn't it odd that a dining room set now makes you realize just how complicated this can be! And why we avoid these uncomfortable conversations, and stick our heads in the sand and procrastinate until it's too late. And let things happen to us when we should be taking charge of them.

Mix in Personality Types—and Stir

I have taken at least a dozen different personality profile tests. My introduction was as an undergrad at Illinois State. I was hired as a tutor by the University Learning Center. One of the things they taught us was how to identify different personalities so we could adjust our teaching style to best suit the student we were working with. I was intrigued. To me, it was like reading the characteristics of your astrological sign, but on steroids.

While earning my MBA, I took classes that specialized in leadership and team building—with more personality profiles! And when I bought my Caring Transitions franchise, there was yet another personality profile. Trust me when I say I am nothing if not self-aware!

Here's what I like about personality profiles. ***The point is not to judge any other personality type, but to understand who you are, so you can better understand others.***

This is really hard to do with your family. Years of emotions make it difficult to see past the hurts and fears, so that you can notice that your parents might have different personality types than yours. They may communicate differently than you do. Imagine how much easier it would be on you if, instead of feeling angry, you were able to understand that mom's mind just works that way. This is going to take some practice.

A Dose of Realism

Be realistic in your expectations of the future. Don't assume that every sibling will play an equal role, or that your mom will be able to live out her days in the family home without ever having to move. Hope for the best but plan for the worst. You have to have a "Plan B."

You are not jinxing everyone by talking about things. You are not bringing about the inevitable any faster by talking and planning for it. You do not have to knock on wood, throw salt over your shoulder or say some magic chant to avoid tempting the Evil Eye.

OK—we are going to do it. We are going to talk! You will sit down with mom discuss her future. Where do you even *begin*?

Choosing a Better Approach

Start with overview types of conversations that won't startle anybody—especially if you've never broached the subject before. Tell mom, dad, and your siblings what you have been thinking about and why. Make sure that your intentions are in the right place and that they know this. That you want to help.

There's an important scene in the Drew Barrymore movie, "Riding in Cars with Boys." Barrymore's now grown child wants to do something that would mean leaving his mother to go off with his girlfriend.

He is talking to his estranged father about this. He believes it will never happen, because his mother won't let go of him emotionally. She needs him too much. The father tells him that, ultimately, his mother just wants to make him happy. Instead of arguing, the way to approach it is to ask for her help. He follows the advice and she immediately moves from arguing to helping.

As you know, it is never going to be as easy as it looks in the movies. But this is a good point: it's all about the approach and viewpoint you create.

Approach can mean everything. It's not about putting your parents in a home—it's about making sure they're safe and cared for. It's not about replacing what the family wants to do to help as dad gets older—it's about making sure they can do so financially. It's not about what you are giving up—it's about maintaining control and making your own decisions while there is still time to investigate options.

Start with the Easy Stuff and Then Gain Momentum

This applies to a lot of things in life. When you learn something new, you don't begin by doing the most difficult thing. The same is true here. Build consensus by starting with the topics you know everyone will agree on, which won't cause arguments or trigger fears.

Be patient. Just because *you* are ready to have a go at this doesn't mean everyone else is. Give them time to digest that you want to talk about topics they may have been avoiding, and then look at what you are proposing.

Using Someone Else's Life

Maybe the father of a friend died suddenly, and her mom now has to move out of the family home because she just can't stay there by herself. Sometimes the caregiver spouse is the one who passes first. Then things become very dire very quickly, as the rest of the family starts to realize just how much dad was doing for mom. Now everyone is scrambling to get mom to a place she can stay on her own.

Using these stories can be a way to break the ice with your own parents without sounding like you are putting them on the spot. Showing empathy toward the family who is now in need—and expressing the desire to avoid a similar experience—can sometimes be the catalyst to get your folks talking if they were previously hesitant. Or to get your brother finally involved in a conversation he has been avoiding. Or even to get yourself off the sidelines.

Does Mom Have a Friend Who Could Help?

There are certain people you mom probably listens to. Maybe there's an aunt or an old friend, or a relative that is not one of her children. Could you gain their assistance? It's just general family dynamics, and we have all seen it. Sometimes you can't carry the message. What is taken as an assault by one person is taken calmly as advice when provided by a different person. This is a very important situation. It may take some legwork to get everyone moving in the same direction.

In my family, this helpful person is Aunt Vicki. Vicki's mom and my mom's mom were sisters. My mom and Aunt Vicki are first cousins and more like sisters. My brother and I tease my mom about whether or not she can get the details to stories straight. It's not a memory problem—she's always been this way. She is the person who makes that childhood game of telephone so hysterical. It is not uncommon at a family dinner for us to look at Vicki when mom tells a story to see if Vicki agrees with the details. Or Vicki will do the same with us.

This is all in good fun. When my mother is truly interested in something, she can get an amazing amount of information perfectly straight with no problem. But if I ever got to the point where I was having trouble getting through to my mom about something I felt was important, the first call I would make would be to Vicki.

Do you have someone in your family's life that can play this role for you?

Read Between the Lines

Don't just ask the questions—listen to the answers. And listen to what is *really* being said. What appears to be a conversation about driving could actually be a conversation about control. When you are talking about potentially moving out of the family home, mom could be thinking about it as mourning the next step in a series of losses that tied her to her family.

Most conversations we have with our aging parents have underlying emotions. These can completely stifle all efforts if they are not acknowledged and addressed.

Remember our earlier conversation about fear? Well it's back, and it's going to derail things in a new variety of ways:

- Dad won't even talk about plans for himself as long as his wife is alive to focus on. He's probably afraid of losing her.

- Mom won't talk about moving into a retirement community. Maybe she is afraid of the change and worried about making new friends.

Fear will complicate your entire effort to talk with your parents. Even the *smallest* amounts of fear will completely override bucket loads of logic. If you do not address the fear, then you probably are not going to get very far.

Oh, and there is a really good chance that nobody is going to *admit* being afraid to you. They're just going to put up wall after wall, and excuse after excuse to avoid the conversations you are trying to have. And it doesn't always come from your parents. It could just as easily come from a sibling.

Key Questions From Chapter 6

- Go in with the right intentions and commit to being the hero in this situation. Ask yourself, "Where is the rest of the family coming from?"

- Be aware of generational differences. Do you know what may have happened in your parents' lives to make them behave the way they do?

- Understand personality differences. Do you know your own personality type's tendencies and those of your parents and/or siblings? How might these differences affect the ability to have uncomfortable conversations?

- Are you being realistic in your approach and your plan?

- Are there other people who could help?

- How is fear affecting the way people are reacting to difficult conversations?

Section 3

WHAT

Now Let's Talk About *What* You
Should Be Talking About

Chapter 7

Who Can Legally Do What

The legal aspects of aging are immense. I work regularly with people as they navigate what should and needs to be done. However, you would benefit from getting an overview of the different issues that are involved from the perspective of an elder law attorney. (Disclaimer time. This is not intended to provide you with personal legal advice! Plus, each state is different, so there may be some nuances you need to double check.) I just know that it is important to provide you with an overview.

So I invited Matt Margolis, of Margolis Weldon, LLC, in Park Ridge, Illinois to join us for a while.

Matt and I met through mutual networking efforts as I was building my Caring Transitions business. Because I have shared some of my stories with you, I will include my favorite story about something that happened when Matt and I first met.

Some years ago, the two of us had our first one-on-one meeting at a local Starbucks. We were being pretty formal and all business-y with each other. Suddenly a beautiful woman rushed through the crowd, kissed Matt on the cheek and rushed back out. He looked a little stunned and embarrassed.

"Who was that?" I asked.

He smiled and said, "My fiancé."

"Does she work around here?"

"Nope."

He later learned that she had to make a stop on her way to work that morning, saw his car in the parking lot, and ran in just to surprise him. That was the first step to my less-formal business relationship with Matt.

The Confusion Over Wills, Trusts and Probate

When it comes to wills and trusts, there is a lot of misunderstanding out there. One is that wills avoid probate (we'll discuss the details of probate later) so we need a will. The other is that trusts are only for "rich" people, or those with a lot more assets than us—whatever *that* means.

I sit down with clients all the time who say, "We don't have that much. We're pretty simple, so we just need a will, right?" When I ask what they have, they respond with, "A house (worth $500,000) a brokerage account (with $750,000), and some other assets valued around $300,000." I love when clients say this, because "not much" to them is usually more than I have... it typically means that their neighbors, the famous Joneses, have more.

The reality is that most people don't know the difference between a will and a trust, what is right for their circumstances, and what probate actually entails. The result is that a lot of people end up in probate many years down the road... well, their family does.

What Does a Will Do?

A will is like formal letter, with lots of legal jargon, meant for a judge to interpret sometime down the road when someone dies. It gives direction on what you want to have happen with all of your "stuff" (again, legal jargon). It names who you want to be in charge (the executor) of making sure your stuff goes to the people you want it to go to (the beneficiaries). And you get to be as simple or complicated as you want. That's really it. The will itself does not help you avoid probate (more on this later). In fact, in most circumstances, it *guarantees* this!

What if mom doesn't have a will? Well, then you're lucky because there's a default to save the day, right? Yes and no. There is a default, but it's not always the one you want. Instead of mom's will (her choices) deciding where her stuff goes, the state's rules come into play and decide all of it for her. In some circumstances, she may get lucky, and the state handles things in the same way that she would have wanted. However, in most cases it isn't.

You know that estranged sister of yours who left home when she was 18 and you haven't spoken to since? Good news: now she gets to inherit some of mom's estate because mom never executed a will, and the state says your sister gets something. Scenarios such as this that can easily be avoided by planning.

What Is Probate?

Probate is the court process that may be involved when we die. If dad didn't choose beneficiaries for his accounts (life insurance, IRAs, 401(k)s, etc.), or pick people who survived him, and he didn't have his assets in some kind of trust, then his estate will likely go through probate when he dies.

In a probate case, the judge is in control and ultimately gets to decide where all of dad's stuff goes (either based on his will or the state's rule book). In most cases, the Executor or the Administrator of his estate (if he didn't have a will) will have to hire an attorney to navigate and handle the probate process. On average, this is likely to take somewhere between nine to 18 months. However, throw in some fights among siblings, and more attorneys getting involved, and this can easily turn into a couple of years. In the end, dad's stuff will go to the beneficiaries (whether he chose them or the state did), but not without some headaches and distress for the family—and usually much less money.

What Is a Revocable Living Trust?

How do you avoid probate? A revocable living trust is the most common type of trust. Friends and family who mention "my trust," most likely have one of these. I like them because they offer protection from probate and are flexible. Changes can be made to them as life goes on.

The trust is a vehicle for us to own our assets (bank and brokerage accounts, stocks, bonds, CDs, annuities, real estate, etc.) and consolidate them. That means when we die, we avoid probate and pass things to our beneficiaries in a detailed and protective way.

What if our children or grandchildren are young when we die? Do we want to give a 17, 18 or even 25-year-old immediate access to potentially large sums of money? We also can provide asset protection to the people who receive money or assets from us in case they are sued or get divorced after we die. We get to "control from the grave" as much or as little as we want.

The bottom line is that our wishes control what happens, and it's done privately. This can be handled within the family or through a banker or trust officer. Either way, we don't have to do it publicly, in a courtroom, over an indefinite period of time.

Who Should Be in Charge of the Trust?

Just as every will has an "executor," every trust has a "trustee." These people play a similar role. They are in charge of making sure that, when the time comes, our assets are being managed appropriately, our expenses are taken care of, and that our beneficiaries receive what we wish.

Sometimes you can name a company to be in charge. When looking at a corporate trustee or executor, you want to consider the value of the estate and that corporation's rules. Does it have a minimum? If it does, you may or may not be able to appoint the company because your estate might be too small for them to handle and, when it comes time, it will decline. What will your estate (or trust) be charged every year to pay for that service? At 4-5 percent per year, that might equate to an annual $10-20,000—no matter how little work is being done. But the corporation has to charge these fees because it is taking on the responsibility of a fiduciary.

Under the law, a fiduciary duty is considered the highest standard of care. A fiduciary is expected to be extremely loyal to the person to whom he owes the duty (the principal). This means there must be no conflict of interest between fiduciary and principal. In cases of executors and trustees, if the fiduciary corporation is negligent in handling the estate or trust, then it can be liable for monetary damages to the beneficiaries.

The other option is to name an individual as your trustee or executor. This should be someone you know very well, whom you trust dearly, and who can be impartial when it's time to distribute assets to your beneficiaries. It could be a spouse, sibling, in-law, trusted advisor (i.e., attorney, CPA, financial advisor/planner, etc.), friend, or adult child.

There's no coincidence that the word "trustee" is used for this person. He or she should be a trustworthy, honest individual. Think about what you have: money, real estate, jewelry, collections, etc. This person will have access to all of it and be in charge of ensuring that it goes where you want.

This is especially important related to a trust, because it's a private process that's not overseen by a judge. I always tell clients there are no "trust police" around to watch this person.

What Are the Different Powers of Attorney?

A common question that I hear from clients, friends, and family is, "Why do I need a power of attorney?" The short answer is because once you turned 18, you became the only person who could make a health care decision on your behalf or sign your own name.

It is important to differentiate between a Power of Attorney for Health Care (HCPOA) and a Power of Attorney for Property (PPOA).

Health Care Power of Attorney

There may come a time when a doctor or other medical professional can't communicate with you about your health care needs, because you are mentally incompetent or physically incapacitated (i.e., in a coma). Then an HCPOA allows someone you legally appoint to talk to the doctor and make a decision on your behalf. This authorized person is called your "agent."

A key component of the HCPOA is that the agent is making *your* decision for you. It is not the agent's decision, or based on how the agent feels about a certain situation. Rather, this person does what you noted in your HCPOA and what you (hopefully) discussed with her or him before you couldn't speak for yourself.

Most powers of attorney for health care allow an individual to note what their wishes are as it relates to life-sustaining treatment.

I'm a huge "Seinfeld" fan, so let's discuss one of the episodes. Kramer meets with his attorney (presumably his estate planning or elder law attorney) and brings his friend Elaine with him. His attorney begins making up different situations in the future where Kramer's health isn't good.

He says: "You're breathing on your own, conscious, but with no muscular function; you have a liver, kidneys, and gall bladder, but no central nervous system; you have one lung, are blind, and eating through a tube; you can eat, but machines do everything else." His asks Kramer whether he would want life support in situations like these. Elaine—the person Kramer is considering appointing as his agent—is giving her opinion on what he should do. In some situations you can see that Kramer agrees, and in others you can see that he doesn't.

I love this episode! The reality is that we will never have the ability to think of every possible scenario we may find ourselves in. The important thing is that we have "the conversation" with the people we are appointing as our agent.

A perfect example of what can go wrong without an HCPOA is the Terry Schiavo case from Florida. In 1990, Schiavo suffered major cardiac arrest. A few months later, she was declared to be in a permanent, vegetative state. In 1998, Schiavo's husband petitioned the court to remove her feeding tube. Her parents opposed this. After many court filings and appeals to the Florida and U.S. Supreme Court, in 2005, the decision to remove the feeding tube was upheld, and she died shortly after this. The problem was that Schiavo did not have an HCPOA in place. That meant no one had the legal authority to instruct the doctors on what to do without court supervision.

Property Power of Attorney

A PPOA allows your legally appointed agent to sign your name on your behalf and to handle your financial affairs.

If you were to become mentally incompetent or physically incapacitated, who would continue to pay your monthly bills so your mortgage is current and your gas and electricity stay on? If you do not have a PPOA in place, no one else has the legal right to access the proper accounts and take care of your financial matters.

What If You Didn't Choose Someone?

If you don't have an HCPOA or PPOA, a legal guardian will be appointed by a court to allow someone to make health care decisions for you, or to legally sign your name. A guardianship is a costly and time-consuming process—made even *more* challenging when the potential ward is not agreeable (typically due to their mental incompetency). This is called a "contested guardianship."

To avoid the potential of any costly and unnecessary court proceedings, consult an attorney to ensure you have valid Powers of Attorney for Health Care and Property in place. This will not only protect *you*, but will save your loved ones a lot of aggravation and expense.

How Does Guardianship Work?

A guardian is appointed by a court and can be authorized to make legal, financial, and health care decisions for the "ward." The guardian may or may not have to seek court approval for decisions that he or she wants to make on behalf of the ward.

There are different standards under which a person is deemed to require a guardian. Like the terms of the guardianship, these are specific to the state where you live. In general, people are "ruled" to be in need of guardianship when they show a lack of capacity to make responsible decisions for themselves. This doesn't mean someone is going to be declared incompetent because he or she makes careless or foolish decisions. The person will be declared incompetent if he or she lacks the capacity to make "sound decisions."

For example, Sally would likely not be declared incompetent just because she spends money in ways that seem weird to others. Similarly, someone with a developmental disability or mental illness is not necessarily going to be called incompetent by a court simply because of their physical or mental character. A judge will typically look at all of the circumstances around how a person makes decisions for him or herself.

In almost every state, anyone interested in another's safety and well-being can request (i.e., petition) a guardianship. In some cases, this person may not need a guardianship at all. But we live in America, where anyone and everyone can bring someone to court for any reason that they think is appropriate (in their own minds).

When a petition for guardianship is filed, it's typically done by an attorney who is hired by the "interested person." The petition will need to be filed in the probate court of the county where the proposed ward lives. During the guardianship proceedings, the ward will have his or her own legal representative so that person's best interests are looked after by a third party. If the proposed ward cannot afford this, then the court will appoint one.

At the guardianship hearing, the court's goal is to determine if this person is incapacitated. If the judge believes this is so, then the court must decide to what extent the person needs help. Once the individual is declared incapacitated, the court must determine if the person who is petitioning for guardianship is suitable for that role. Is the person responsible, honest, trustworthy, solvent, mentally stable, etc.?

The court must be very careful in "vetting" this person, to make sure he or she will be an appropriate guardian. The last thing it wants to do is appoint someone who ends up taking advantage of or not taking care of the ward.

A guardian can be any competent adult. Typically, the first route would be a family member. What happens if the ward doesn't have any family that is living, appropriate, or willing? Then a friend, neighbor, or a professional guardian is appointed. In some situations, a guardian is not a person at all. It can be a non-profit organization, or a public or private corporation.

In appointing a guardian, courts give precedence to people who are close to the ward. The idea is that these people will likely know things about the ward that most others wouldn't. This may be likes/dislikes, emotional reactions, personality traits and behaviors, and the ward in general. If this were me, I would want someone who knows and cares about me to make the right decisions for me.

Many states distinguish between guardians that will be in charge of making different types of decisions for the ward. One will be responsible for financial and property-related decisions, and the other makes health care decisions. In some cases, this can be the same person.

Courts will often give guardians broad power to take care of the ward, as long as whatever they're doing is in the ward's best interests.

With this said, there is obviously the potential for a guardian to abuse his or her power (neglecting the health and welfare of the ward or stealing from the ward). For these reasons, courts hold guardians accountable for their actions. Most courts require the guardian of the estate to appear at least annually to "check in" and give inventories of the ward's assets and accounts. In many situations, the guardian for the estate must get approval from the court before making certain financial transactions. The court wants to ensure the person it appointed is doing everything that he or she promised to do from the start.

Guardians will often have to offer proof that they have made reasonable living arrangements for the ward and that adequate health care services and treatment have been provided. Those who fail to prove that they have adequately cared for the person in their charge may be removed and replaced by another guardian.

Thanks Matt!

Key Questions From Chapter 7

- Do you need a will or a trust? Are your documents in order to prevent a prolonged, family-wrenching probate process?

- Who should be in charge of the will or trust being executed?

- Are the right people in place for your HCPOA and PPOA to perform your wishes as desired and not decide them for you?

Chapter 8

Finding Money to Support Your Parents—and You

This chapter may be more helpful for *you* than anything related to your parents!

As we discussed in Chapter 3, waiting reduces options and makes them more expensive. If you haven't started having those uncomfortable conversations with your parents, it might be a bit too late for some of these options. But it's not too late for *you!*

None of the information I share with you here replaces what you should do by sitting down with your financial planner. My goal isn't to tell you the "right option." Instead, it's to remind you that the earlier you plan the more options you have. Here are some of them.

Annuities Made Easy

Annuities are a way to insure that you won't run out of money as you get older.

There are several types of annuities and several ways that you can pay for them. You may put in one lump sum of money, or you can make payments into them over time. Annuities can earn interest in a variety of ways. You may purchase different "riders" that give you other benefits you might want. There are even a number of ways to collect your money from an annuity.

In very general terms, the point of an annuity is to provide a stream of money back to a designated person.

One of the complaints about annuities is that they are illiquid – meaning that they are hard to "undo" if needed.

A Quick Look at Long-Term Care Insurance

Even though long-term care insurance (LTCi) is something people associate with seniors, you are unlikely to qualify for if you wait too long to apply.

LTCi covers the costs of *custodial* care, versus the *skilled* care that is covered by health insurance (and, eventually, Medicare). Custodial care has to do with things that are not going to improve. It's not the physical therapy that will help you walk again after a hip replacement. Instead, it's the help with bathing and dressing you need if you can't do these things for yourself, and your doctor expects your situation to stay that way for at least six months.

We have already talked about how people live longer than they used to. And even though they are generally healthier for a longer time, the increase in longevity is bringing a greater need for assistance.

There have been a few times in this book where I have asked you to stop a moment and notice a particular point. Here's another one.

The lack of understanding of this *huge* gap in financial planning has devastating effects on the families with a parent needing long-term care assistance. It is the difference between making sure mom has the best care available to her, and having to settle for what the government says she can have. It is the difference between sound financial decision-making, and potential financial ruin as you commit to ensuring mom has the best care— even if you can't technically afford it. And it is the difference between mom leaving any financial legacy to her grandchildren, and having to spend it all in the final years of her life.

Genworth Financial is one of the leading LTCi companies in the country. Each year, it publishes a study on the average costs of care in each state. It is freely available. If you want to give yourself a heart attack, take a minute to look it up online and peek at your state's averages.

In the 2014 Cost of Care study, Genworth found that the national *median cost* for an assisted living community was $42,000 a year. Don't just assume the costs are greater only in those areas that are traditionally higher to live in, such as New York or Chicago or Los Angeles. Sometimes the costs are higher than average because of the limited options in the area.

Use this information to estimate what costs might be when *you* may need to be looking at your options. Then talk with your financial planner about how to cover these costs.

Hybrid Life Insurance Summary

One of the most common objections to purchasing LTCi is, "What if I never use it?" This always seemed a bit odd to me. I never heard of any other insurance products that people were disappointed *not* to use. Nobody is upset they didn't need to use their homeowner's insurance, or their car insurance…

A hybrid life/long-term care policy is one answer to this. I won't get into the different types of life insurance that are available now, but I do want to point out that several of them come with what is called an accelerated death benefit. This means you can access the money from the life insurance policy, under specific conditions, to help pay for the costs of care while you are still alive.

The policies are designed so that there is some remaining death benefit available to heirs although it will be a lower amount. More importantly, to those of you who are concerned about not using the long-term care portion of the plan, your heirs will receive more money if you don't need to tap into that benefit.

Checking Your Own Facts

Remember the ducks from the introduction? Are you sure yours are in a row?

In Chapter 3, I mentioned how planning is not a "one and done" situation. Of course you should review the legal and financial documents you have created to make sure the directives they outline are what you still want. However, there is another very important reason to take a regular look: accuracy.

You would be amazed—and probably terrified—by all the inaccuracies in documents that have long ago been filed away. Nobody notices these errors until it's time to make a change.

An Old Story That Can Help Your Future

In 1999, we were all planning for January 1, 2000, to be the end of the technology we relied on. Everyone I knew was having a complete meltdown over what would happen to the calendar on their computer when it tried to flip over to the new year. The consensus was that no computer existed that could handle the change, and we were going to find ourselves thrown overnight into the Mad Max post-apocalyptic world of no electricity. Maybe that is an exaggeration, but that is certainly how it felt to us in corporate jobs, as directive after directive came down from the chief information officer.

About a year before the anticipated end of the world, my husband at the time and I bought new cell phones. We paid my portion of the bill and his portion was reimbursed to us by his company. We saved money by having our phones linked together.

His company required a letter from the phone company stating it was Y2K compliant. (Remember that?) The company doesn't exist anymore, so naming it won't be a problem. It was Primeco—the one with the little pink alien mascot. So my husband called Primeco to ask for this letter. In 1999, you still more often then not got to talk to a human being instead of an automated teller, so a person actually answered the phone. She told my husband that his account information was inaccurate, so she could not help him.

He called me. I called Primeco. I also was told that my account information was inaccurate so the company couldn't provide me with a Y2K compliant letter.

Now both of us have "inaccurate account information." However, our phones worked fine and Primeco had no problem accepting our money each month. Within the week—and at least a dozen increasingly irate phone calls later—our account was "red flagged." We had become problem customers, and nobody would help us. And we were on the verge of losing our phone bill reimbursement because nobody would give us a letter of compliance, and nobody could figure out why we were such a problem.

I finally went into the store and convinced a nice person to let me browse our contact information. I noticed that when we purchased the phones, the store's customer service representative had completely mixed up our names, birthdays and social security numbers. So of course when we were calling and confirming our identities, these came up wrong. And because we could not predict how Primeco had mixed and matched our information, we couldn't fix it.

While a ridiculously annoying situation, in the grand scheme of things it didn't really have much consequence. But what if the mix and match mess up is on your list of beneficiaries for your IRA—and because everything is entered into a computer nobody knows exactly where the error is? And then, in the end, when you should be focusing on grieving, you have to run around, trying to figure out this crazy impossible puzzle that could have been avoided by taking a regular look at your documents.

I have an associate who has a business that reviews financial documents for people and gets these organized. I call her a "financial planner paralegal." She tells me that she has never in all her years in business brought on a single client who did not have at least one error in their paperwork. Terrifying!

It's Not the Golden Years but the Rusty Years

My 97-year-old aunt likes to say to me, "It ain't easy getting old!" She is right. Well, unfortunately, it is not cheap either!

I hope you will not be in a situation where you require public assistance. However, I would be remiss if I didn't address the forms of public help available to help people with the costs of aging.

Medicaid (Courtesy of Matt)

Medicaid is the federally mandated program administered by each state, according to its specific rules and regulations. This program provides benefits for individuals at home and in certain facilities. It is a needs-based benefit, which has specific requirements related to individuals' asset levels and income. These numbers vary, depending on the state.

When you apply for Medicaid before moving into a nursing home, there are also rules about giving away your assets as gifting within a certain period before you submit your application (i.e., a "look back" period). In many situations, this becomes the trickiest of the rules, because what is considered a "gift"? The Medicaid definition of "gift" is the "transfer of assets for less than fair market value."

Let's look at a few examples:

- I gave $14,000 to each of my children last year because the IRS said I could.

This is a gift, even though the IRS says it's OK. The IRS allows us to give a certain amount of money each year to everyone we know. We don't need to tell the IRS, and this doesn't come off of our "lifetime coupon" as it relates to estate and gift taxes. However, IRS and Medicaid rules are different, so this is a "no-no" for purposes of Medicaid qualification.

- I paid for part of my grandson's college tuition for the last three years.

  This is extremely thoughtful and something a lot of grandparents want to do to help their grandchildren. But Medicaid will consider it a gift because there isn't anything being received for fair market value (even though every grandparent would argue otherwise).

- I took my name off the deed to my house and put my children's names on it.

  This is 100 percent a gift. This is directly giving away the value of one's house to another person. It doesn't matter that it's the person's children.

- I sold my car to my daughter for $3,000 even though it was worth $17,000.

  Part of this is a gift and part of it isn't. The $3,000 isn't a gift, but the $14,000 difference between the fair market value and the sale price is.

It's imperative that you become educated about Medicaid's rules and regulations before doing an application. There are the rules, and then there are the exceptions—and even "loopholes" in some situations. Some states have allowances related to transferring assets to children and grandchildren that are *not* considered gifts. However, there are very particular ways in which the transfers need to occur and circumstances that must happen to do so (the existence of a disability, special needs, or other). A visit with an elder law attorney can help you decipher what the options are based on your specific circumstances.

Veteran's Administration Aid

Here's a common question I hear: "Are there any benefits, other than Medicaid, to help pay for my dad's care?" This is typically asked because Medicaid (the "long-term care version") is only available for someone in a skilled nursing facility or supportive living facility. My follow-up question to them is usually, "Are your dad or mom veterans?"

If so, I discuss the Veterans Administration's (VA) Aid and Attendance pension with them. In most situations, people have never heard of this benefit. It's actually classified as a "pension" by the VA. This is a great source of funds for financially constrained wartime veterans and/or their surviving spouses. They may use it for their long-term care costs, such as living at home with a caregiver, adult day care, independent living with a caregiver, assisted living, and/or skilled nursing.

Family income is one of the determining factors for eligibility. It also is important to know that the VA allows individuals to deduct their unreimbursed medical expenses—health insurance premiums, home care, assisted living, adult day care, caregiver, and nursing home costs—from their income. As a result, many Veterans who may not have previously qualified might do so now if long-term care has become necessary for them or their spouse.

As a general rule, to qualify for the Aid and Attendance benefit, a family's total assets (excluding their primary residence and vehicles) can't exceed $80,000. Fortunately, many of my clients have more than this. The good news is that, with the right strategies and planning, we can still position them to qualify. Just as with Medicaid applications, it makes sense to meet with an elder law attorney when looking into applying for this benefit.

Currently this benefit (unlike Medicaid), has no look back period as far as gifting/transferring assets is concerned. This means gifts are not prohibited. However, recently proposed legislation is calling for a look back period, which would negatively affect a veteran (or surviving spouse). In 2015, the benefit ranges from a little over $1,100 per month for the surviving spouse of a veteran, to a little over $2,100/month for a veteran with a dependent (typically a spouse). And the benefit is tax-free.

In the end, the VA Aid and Attendance pension is a heavily untapped, but much-deserved benefit for those veterans who served and fought for our country and their surviving spouses.

Key Questions From Chapter 8

- There are many financial products that can help you plan for the costs of aging. Are you working with someone who can help determine which ones are right for you?

- Will you need long-term care insurance? This covers the costs of helping with activities of daily living—not with getting better.

- Are you regularly reviewing all of your documents to make sure they are up-to-date and have accurate details?

- Are you aware of any public benefits you may qualify for or how to access them?

Chapter 9

Where Do You Call Home?

In 1954, the first age-restricted community was created in Youngstown, Arizona. Since then, the variety of options designed to give the aging population choices for living has exploded. Here is an outline of some of the many options you have.

Aging in Place, aka Staying Home

Most parents will tell you that they want to stay in their home for the rest of their lives. There are many factors involved in how this could be more difficult—and yet more possible—than it used to be.

More and more, families no longer live geographically close to each other. This can make staying at home more difficult for an aging parent. It used to be very common for at least one of the children to move back into the family home once their parents started aging and their own nuclear family got bigger: especially after the death of one of their parents.

And while your mom may be willing to live with you and your family, you may now live across the country from where you grew up. This means that mom would have to leave her friends and her own social world to stay with you. And remember the fear we were talking about before: how much *more* frightening is it to move out of the home you have been in for 50 years when that move also involves a 2,000-mile adjustment.

The type of home and climate where you live can have a huge impact on how possible it is to stay at home and for how long. Here in Chicago, even if mom lives in a single-story ranch so there are no stairs to worry about, you still have the snow, and ice and temperatures that can trap even the most durable of us in our homes for months. Of course there are services that will remove the snow for you, but bundling up and driving to/ from the grocery store and doctors' appointments can become downright life-threatening at times.

Services to Help People Stay at Home

If staying at home is the right choice, there is plenty of support available.

Home health care agencies provide a variety of assistance that will go a long way toward allowing dad to stay at home as long as possible. Here are the most common services:

- Companion

- Meal preparation

- Personal care, such as bathing and dressing

- Transportation

- Help with household duties

One thing I really appreciate about home health care services—which I never hear anyone make a big deal of—is walking your mom's dog while they are there. Again, especially in inclement weather, trekking out with even a small dog can be a dangerous thing. The benefit of being able to keep your dog because someone is there to walk it is priceless!

There are a lot of other services that can help keep mom at home that you might not ordinarily think of. Getting a little help with some of these activities reduces the risk of falls and injuries. While some of these may be obvious, others should give you some fresh ideas:

- House cleaning

- Snow removal/lawn maintenance

- Dog walker (keeping pets is very important!)

- Professional organizer/bill payer (This is not a financial planner but someone who can help organize and pay monthly bills, and continue to help if mom decides to move into independent living.)

- Emergency alert systems—such as for falls

- Caption telephones

- Transportation services

You may look at some of these items and say to yourself, "I can handle these." That's great. I'm not suggesting that you replace what the family is already able to do. Just to take a minute to think of options and alternatives that allow mom to remain independent and in control.

This is particularly helpful when it comes to driving. I can't tell you how many times I've seen an argument over mom keeping her driver's license completely stop when the idea of a private driver is offered to mom instead. Remember: it's all in how you approach it. Give something instead of taking something away.

Again, this service can happen at home or at an independent living community. While many communities and even public neighborhoods have special transportation services for seniors, there is nothing quite like mom telling her friends, "My driver is waiting for me."

Adult Day Care

Adult day care can often be found as a program within an assisted or independent living community, or as a stand-alone service within the neighborhood's community or senior center. But, seriously, someone needs to come up with a better name!

Many families I work with just talk about it as "going to the club."

These options are great when mom lives with you, but everyone is gone during the day. She needs some care but also wants social engagement. Or when mom is dad's primary caregiver and needs some rest and time to herself while dad goes to "the club" a few times a week.

Since I brought it up, let's take a minute to consider the implications of aging parents being each other's primary caregiver. This is a very common situation and important to pay attention to.

The most frequent approach is mom taking care of dad—sometimes at the risk of and detriment to her own health. Using any of the stay-at-home or adult day care services is going to have a profound impact on keeping mom healthier longer. You can't exaggerate the impact that full-time caregiving has on a person, especially people who may be experiencing their own age-related issues.

Here's the tricky part. Your parents are so bound to each other that the guilt you had to deal with when considering hiring simple household help for mom tasks *pales in comparison* to trying to get mom to accept some assistance with dad. It's been her job for upwards of 50 years!

I am stopping you again to make an important point! *This is all in the approach.* Nobody is trying to replace what mom does. We are just trying to help her do it for longer.

This is one of those times we talked about before. When conversations aren't going to be easy. When you may have to have the talk several times to reach an agreement. When deep emotions are involved. Don't give up. It's too important.

Age Restricted Community

Age Restricted Communities are built for adults who remain active and want the options of having amenities without competing with young families for access. They can be large, spread-out subdivisions with club-houses, or in urban areas, a single condominium building.

While they exist everywhere, many of these communities are in warmer climates. Often they are the second home of "snowbirds" who decide they don't want to give up their homes "up north" near their families, but they no longer need to be subjected to the harsh winters.

While there are often extensive amenities onsite—such as pools, clubhouses and golf courses—each person or couple owns their own home or condominium, and it looks like any other neighborhood in the area.

Independent Living Community

Independent Living Communities are for people and couples who want to live independently but don't want to be responsible for the upkeep of an entire home. They would like to have fewer things to worry about.

These communities are often located in a single building, so residents do not have to go outside during bad weather to get to any of the amenities. They also provide meals and light housekeeping. Financially, these can either be a buy-in condominium model or a monthly rental.

Many of the services your parents would want also are available within the building. These often include hair salons, banks and even a variety of medical-related specialists, such as an eye doctor or physical therapist. While everyone is expected to be able to live independently, having these services nearby allows them to do so.

There is also a huge social aspect to these communities.

This is one of those points where I waiver back and forth about what is best for someone. I completely understand the desire to stay at home for as long as possible. But I also see the amazing benefit of moving to a community that will provide a great improvement in quality of life.

Too often I see people so tied to the "stay at home at all costs" idea that they give up the social interaction and benefits of being with others. Is staying at home alone with 12 hours a day of television really how you want your mom to be spending her last years?

The idea of "use it or lose it" comes into play here. There's no one answer that's right for every person. But I have personally seen an improvement in health and mental capacity in people who have chosen—after a long period of solitude at home—to move into a thriving community where they are being provided with regular healthy meals and social interaction.

A financial note: Long-term care insurance will *not* pay for the rent at an Independent Living Community. However, it may pay for some of the additional services there. In addition, paying for those services yourself could go toward the elimination period required for benefits to start. If you have a long-term care policy, make sure you are documenting access to it properly.

Assisted Living Communities

Assisted Living Communities provide extensive day-to-day assistance for their residents. It is assumed that the people who live there may require help getting dressed, bathing, feeding themselves, etc.

While there is often a choice between staying home and moving to an independent living community, that choice becomes less feasible as more care is needed. The costs and the safety factors involved in trying to keep dad at home end up making the decision for you. But this still does not make them the same as what you would think of as a nursing home. In a good Assisted Living Community, much effort is taken to create a home environment and not a clinical one.

Continuing Care Retirement Communities (CCRC)

CCRCs often are the most expensive version of a long-term living plan, but they have some great benefits as well. An initial buy-in is required, as well as monthly fees (depending on the level of care needed). Many people believe the benefit of the CCRC model is that all potential levels of needed care are available within the one community—although not necessarily in one building or one floor. The idea is that another dramatic move outside of your mom's home here will be avoided, and you won't have to worry about additional housing decisions as mom's care level changes.

Long-term care insurance will *not* pay for the rent of the unit in the independent living side of a CCRC, or for the buy in. That does not mean, however, that it won't eventually kick in to pay some benefits as needs of care change.

During one of my days at the long-term care insurance brokerage firm, I answered the phone to find a client asking me about her LTCi policy. She had it for more than 10 years and was wondering if she could get any of her premiums back if she cancelled it. I asked why she would want to cancel it after so long. She told me her financial advisor said she didn't need it anymore because she was moving into a CCRC and they would be taking care of everything. Then she told me she was just mere days from the policy being cancelled for non-payment of premium.

No-No-*No!*

As I mentioned, your LTCi policy will not cover the buy in, or the rent, or many of the service charges when you first move into the independent living side of a CCRC. Once benefits are triggered, however, as you need more care, then the policy will absolutely cover appropriate charges.

A CCRC does not mean you have no more fees except your rent. And even if the bill is provided to you as all-inclusive, the community can help you identify which charges can be covered by your policy. Do not waste the premium you have paid by letting a policy lapse because you are moving into a CCRC! And do not let the fact that you have been paying premiums on a policy keep you from deciding to move into a CCRC.

Medicaid Facilities

Let's face it: the costs of housing as you age are very expensive, and not all of us will have the means to privately pay for the care our parents need. And too many of us either avoided having uncomfortable conversations, or couldn't get our parents to participate in them. And maybe our family isn't one of those that is really good at planning. So we may need government assistance when it comes time for dad to have to move out of the house.

Across the country, there are facilities where care is paid for by Medicaid. To qualify for Medicaid to pay for your long-term care needs, mom can't be able to care for herself at home, and she must not be able to pay for the care she needs.

The costs of care are going up. The population in general is aging. The bills the government already has on its hands is growing by leaps and bounds. As a result, qualifying for Medicaid already has—and no doubt will continue to become—more difficult.

In addition to the qualification process, not all of the different housing options we previously discussed will accept Medicaid payments. In fact, most won't. Communities and facilities that are funded primarily via Medicaid are generally not as robust as those that receive private payments or funds from long-term care insurance.

On the northern side of Illinois, we are pretty lucky because there are some very nice Medicaid facilities with some amazing staff who genuinely want to do the best for their residents. Unfortunately, these facilities can have extremely long waiting lists. And often when it comes time to move out of the family home, waiting is the last thing you are able to do.

Nationwide, there is a push to improve Medicaid facilities as well. The Nursing Home Quality Initiative was started in 2002 by the Center for Medicare and Medicaid Services. It is charged with providing consumer and provider information about nursing homes.

Much about a Medicaid facility reminds me of the rest of what we have discussed. The idea is to plan for the future so that mom can keep control over the decisions that affect her. Often, relying on Medicaid to pay for care as you age means giving control away. You end up going wherever they decide to put you when you need to move.

Hospice

Hopefully you have read this book well before your parents are anywhere near the end of their lives. My intent was to help you plan for their future, not wait until the near end to see what you could have done. Also, my wish is to give you good food for thought on your own aging.

That being said, let's talk about hospice care. It's related to our subject and, even if you didn't get to talk to your aging parents about each step of their journey, this is a service that can still provide some assistance.

Hospice workers are my heroes (followed closely by dementia patient caregivers). I can't imagine a more emotionally difficult role then as a guide through the final steps of someone's life.

Hospice is the care provided to terminally ill patients that addresses their pain and emotional symptoms. It is not about getting better. It is about making sure the desires of the patient are not lost in our society's drive to focus solely on "fixing things."

Key Questions From Chapter 9

- One of the most important questions you can ask your parents is, "Where do you want to live if you can no longer live at home?"

- Being able to stay at home can involve a variety of services. Are you being proactive about it?

- What are you doing to be prepared to balance the benefits of moving with the desire to stay home?

Conclusion

Love and Good Intentions Go a Long Way

I keep trying to remember what some of my most uncomfortable conversations were. I have only vague memories of the conversation with my mother about the birds and the bees. Mostly I remember being in fourth grade when she gave me the book, *Where Did I Come From?* I imagine those were some uncomfortable conversations for her. I have no idea what occurred between either of my parents and my brother on that subject, but I know he got the same book!

There were the times my parents had to tell us that a grandparent had passed. Those were rough. But these conversations had an immediacy that couldn't be avoided. The same thing happened when my mom told us that she and my dad were getting divorced. I don't know how long they knew before they spoke to us. I'm sure my mom was not looking forward to that conversation but, again, a deadline loomed that couldn't be put off.

Later in life, telling my then-husband that I wanted a divorce is way up on top of the list of conversations I was absolutely terrified of having. To be so hurt that I knew I had to make that move—and to know it was going to hurt someone I loved as well—was really hard. It took two years of feeling things might be heading that way before being able to have that conversation. This was followed by about four months between making the decision in my heart and then acting on it. I don't know that delay cost me anything more than additional heartache. But preserving my long-term friendship with my now ex-husband was more important to me than rushing through anything.

Giving my notice at the LTCi brokerage firm was also a difficult conversation for me. It was the right decision for my future, but I was very close with my associates and, in particular, my bosses and mentors.

Remembering these examples, I notice that they *all* involved people whom I loved and who loved me. And because the approach was done right, and with the best intentions, the results have all been positive.

When I think about having the different conversations with my parents as they age, I am not nearly as uncomfortable as I was in these other instances. Every family has its own version of dysfunction. For mine, the one thing that is *not* a problem is having blunt conversations with each other. Writing this book was a very good reminder that what may be easy in one category of my life may not be so easy in others. While I am confident in my ability to have uncomfortable conversations with my aging parents, I'm using this book as a reminder to look at other parts of my life where I may be avoiding similar situations—and what that is costing me.

You Can't Make This Stuff Up

My mom just called. I am about 90 percent done with this book, just finalizing the layout and working on a few places where I want to beef up the stories or the key points.

She said she has decided to sell the family home in Chicago and buy a small condo for when she is in town, and then move from her small place in Florida to a larger house there. Basically, she'll make Florida her permanent residence. It's weird. She's talking about the house I grew up in. The house she took three jobs at once after her divorce to keep. It's a bigger deal to her than to me. After all, it was her struggle to keep it, and the first house that she ever lived in, and where she raised her family.

I'm more transient. I have moved fairly often, although that house has always been home base. It is the home that houses all my memories.

This is the right decision—no matter how difficult a one. Why pay to keep the larger house in Chicago, with the heating bill and the snow removal, when you plan on being in Florida for those months anyway?

Would it be nice to have a house to pass on to my brother or me? It doesn't really matter. My brother and his family have their own beautiful home, and my mother's house is more space than I would want for myself—even with the little zoo I have collected. Plus, she needs the money to purchase the new house in Florida. And she needs to properly invest the rest of the proceeds to pay for her care as she ages.

I will have my ups and downs as we go through the process (and it *will* be a process) of deciding what to do with all the stuff that has accumulated over the years.

But here's the point. It's a difficult situation, yet nobody is burying their head in the sand. My mother made the decision, and it's the right one for her. We will all work together to make it happen, because that's what you do with your family.

Where to Go for More Help

There is nothing more frustrating then coming to terms with a difficulty and deciding wholeheartedly to move forward taking care of it—and then not knowing what to do.

Here are two additional groups of people who could help you as you work with your aging parents on planning their futures: elder law attorneys and geriatric care managers.

Elder Law Attorney

Once more from Matt: Elder law attorneys concentrate their practices on many various areas of the law. They can include the preservation/transfer of assets when applying for Medicaid, Medicare claims and appeals, Social Security and disability claims and appeals, disability planning, conservatorships and guardianships, estate planning, probate and administration of estates, nursing home issues, elder abuse and fraud recovery cases, and mental health law, to name a few.

Most elder law attorneys do *not* specialize in all of these areas. So it's important to inquire what their focus is and if your issue is in their "wheel house." Hopefully, the attorney will give you an honest answer.

An elder law attorney (and his or her staff) should not only be familiar with the legal issues in helping seniors or those with disabilities. This person should also be compassionate, warm, and be there to "hold the hands" of their clients and families. A lot of the issues that clients bring to them involve sickness, chronic medical conditions, disability, financial distress, and death. The attorney should have good "bedside manner" no different than a geriatric physician.

It's common for an elder law attorney to have a wide circle of professionals who are trusted resources for his or her clients. This can include nursing homes, assisted living facilities, supportive living facilities, caregiving companies (companion care and medical), estate sale companies, senior move managers, real estate agents, dentists, reverse mortgage specialists, nurses, social workers, geriatric care managers, financial advisors and planners, accountants, doctors, long term care specialists, and individuals who can assist seniors with bill paying and managing their finances. They do this because, in many cases, the attorneys might not be the right people to solve the problem, or the potential client would be best suited taking care of some other need first before working with them.

Because elder law is a more commonly known practice area today, many people may find that their friends and family have had a good experience working with an elder law attorney and can give you a referral. If this isn't the case, then here are some great places you may consider asking: nursing homes and other senior living facilities, geriatric care managers, discharge planners at hospitals, an area agency (or council) on aging, or National Academy of Elder Law Attorneys (NAELA).

Geriatric Care Managers (GCM)

A GCM can help your family with the needs your parents may be facing, including referrals and recommendations to resources in your community. Often they have a background including but not limited to nursing, gerontology or social work. This means a care manager can help put specific steps in place to care for you parents or act as a patient advocate on their behalf.

In particular, I have found a GCM to be of even greater assistance when the rest of the family no longer lives in the same geographic area as their aging parents.

Do the Right Thing—and the Best You Can

If you've gotten this far in the book, then you know you need to do this.

Commit to yourself that you'll start having these conversations. Gather your resources—and your courage. Give it a go. Mess up. Take a deep breath and try again.

No matter how hard this feels—and whatever drama it churns up in your family—it still will be less awful than if you did nothing.

If mom dies with an outdated will and you don't know what her real wishes were. If dad outlives his money and gets shuttled among members of the family. If you and your siblings end up in shouting matches because someone feels overburdened with mom's care and the others aren't stepping up.

You are giving a gift to your parents, family, and yourself in facing these matters, rather than avoiding them because things feel uncomfortable. And you are showing the people who may end up as your caregivers how *you* want to be treated as you get older.

You need to do this. And now you're ready. Good luck.

A Note From the Author

In 2012, after a 12-year career at a long-term care insurance broker-age firm, I opened a Caring Transitions office in the north suburbs of Chicago that focuses on senior relocation and estate liquidation. It has grown very well over the past years and oftentimes, while my team did the physical work we were hired for, I found myself sitting at the kitchen table, usually with mom and the oldest daughter, basically talking them off the ledge. Between my activities to grow my Caring Transitions business and my previous career in long-term care insurance, I had all sorts of information I could share with my clients about what they needed to be prepared for in the years to come.

With my pragmatic approach, empathetic and casual conversation demeanor, and strong belief in personal responsibility, I was able to express to my clients how important planning for the future is as we age, how much we stand to lose if we don't do it, how to go about it and what should be discussed.

While we certainly provide a great service with the tasks that we perform for clients, personally I experienced an even greater satisfaction when I knew I made a bigger impact on their lives. I began to realize the message I have to share is bigger and more important than just what I know about helping an aging parent downsize.

Once this realization hit me I knew I had to act on it.

I had to deliver this message to more then just my Chicago-based clients. I have to make people understand that the lack of planning for the future of aging parents—and then their own future—is going to cost them in financial and emotional ways that they can't even imagine.

It's actually about maintaining control over your future—not giving up your independence. Coming from someone as fiercely independent as I am, this is a very important distinction.

So I wrote this book.

For even more information on ways I can help you plan for the future of your aging parents, please visit my website: www.ErinMarcus.com